The Jonas Brothers
Rock Stars

Maggie Murphy

PowerKiDS press™

New York

To Leah Forbes

Published in 2011 by The Rosen Publishing Group, Inc.
29 East 21st Street, New York, NY 10010

First Edition

Book Design: Greg Tucker
Photo Researcher: Jessica Gerweck

Photo Credits: Cover Dan MacMedan/WireImage/Getty Images; p. 5 Ray Tamarra/Getty Images; pp. 6–7, 9, 10–11, 13, 19 Rob Hoffman/ JBE/Getty Images; pp. 14–15 Joe Kohen/Getty Images; pp. 16–17 Ferdaus Shamim/WireImage/Getty Images; p. 21 Gareth Davies/Getty Images; pp. 22–23 Tyrone Kerr/FilmMagic/Getty Images.

Library of Congress Cataloging-in-Publication Data

Murphy, Maggie.
  The Jonas Brothers : rock stars / Maggie Murphy.
     p. cm. — (Young and famous)
  Includes index.
  ISBN 978-1-4488-0646-1 (library binding.) —
ISBN 978-1-4488-1805-1 (pbk.) — ISBN 978-1-4488-1806-8 (6-pack)
  1. Jonas Brothers—Juvenile literature. 2. Rock musicians—United States—Biography—Juvenile literature. I. Title.
  ML3930.J62M87 2011
  782.42164092'2—dc22
  [B]
                         2009050110

Manufactured in the United States of America

CPSIA Compliance Information: Batch #WS10PK: For Further Information contact Rosen Publishing, New York, New York at 1-800-237-9932

Contents

The Jonas Brothers are rock stars. They live in Los Angeles, California.

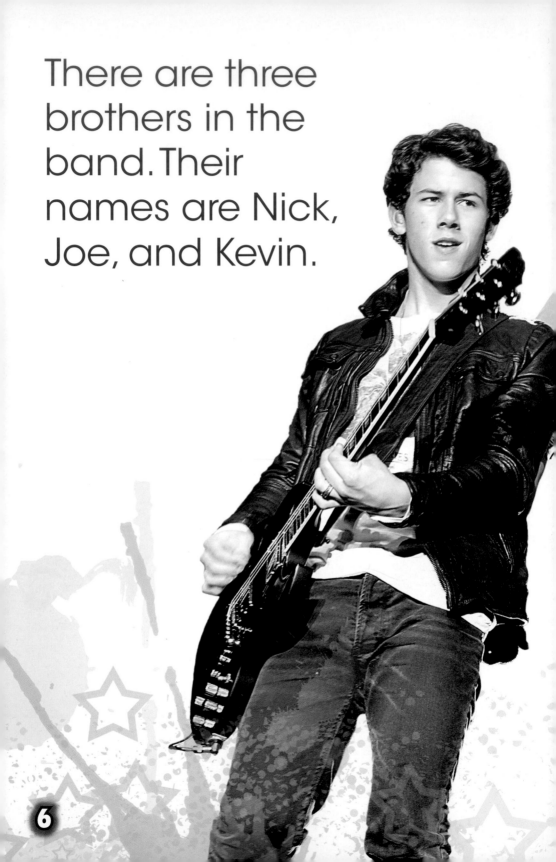

There are three brothers in the band. Their names are Nick, Joe, and Kevin.

Kevin is the oldest.
He plays the guitar
and sings.

Joe is the **middle** brother. He is **famous** for his singing.

Nick is the youngest. He sings and plays the guitar, keyboard, and drums.

The Jonas Brothers are **actors**, too. They are on a TV show called *JONAS*.

They also star in the *Camp Rock* movies.

The Jonas Brothers play **concerts** often.

They have many fans.
Their fans love their
music and acting.

The Jonas Brothers will make music for years to come.

Books

Here are more books to read about the Jonas Brothers:

Johns, Michael-Anne. *Just Jonas! The Jonas Brothers Up Close and Personal.* Star Scene. New York: Scholastic, Inc., 2008.

Rawson, Katherine. *The Jonas Brothers.* Kid Stars! New York: PowerKids Press, 2010.

Web Sites

Due to the changing nature of Internet links, PowerKids Press has developed an online list of Web sites related to the subject of this book. This site is updated regularly. Please use this link to access the list:
www.powerkidslinks.com/young/jb/

Glossary

actors (AK-turz) People who play parts in plays, movies, or TV shows.

concerts (KONT-serts) Public musical performances.

famous (FAY-mus) Very well known.

middle (MIH-dul) Halfway between two things.

Index